Under Col

Life in a nineteenth-century silk factory

**Carol Adams, Paula Bartley,
Judy Lown, Cathy Loxton**

Cambridge University Press

*London   New York   New Rochelle
Melbourne   Sydney*

Published by the Press Syndicate of the University of Cambridge
The Pitt Building, Trumpington Street, Cambridge CB2 1RP
32 East 57th Street, New York, NY 10022, USA
10 Stamford Road, Oakleigh, Melbourne 3166, Australia

First published 1983
Reprinted 1985

Printed in Great Britain by the University Press, Cambridge

Library of Congress catalogue card number: 83–7500

British Library cataloguing in publication data

Under control: life in a nineteenth-century silk factory.
(Women in history)
1. Silk manufacture and trade – Halstead (Essex) – History – 19th century – Case studies
I. Adams, Carol   II. Series
338.4′7677391242′09426715   HD9921.8.M3

ISBN 0 521 27481 8

Maps by Reg Piggott

Portrait drawings by Ian Newsham

The authors and publisher would like to thank the
following for permission to reproduce illustrations:
Front cover, pp. 13, 14 (below), 15 (above and
below left), 16, 20 Courtaulds PLC; Title page, pp.
17, 32 Essex County Records.

A note on money in this book

£1 = 20s (shillings)
1s = 12d (pence)
The old shilling has become 5 new pence.
Remember that the value of money was very
different in the nineteenth century. To work out the
real value you should compare the wages people
received with how much they had to pay for food,
rent, etc.

Contents

Authors' acknowledgement

We should like to thank the following for their generous help:

Mr Cross, Halstead and District Local History Society
Courtauld PLC
Essex Record Office
University of Essex Library
Fred Brown, retired Courtaulds foreman
The students of Lewisham and Malory schools

This book is based upon research that Judy Lown has been doing since 1976.

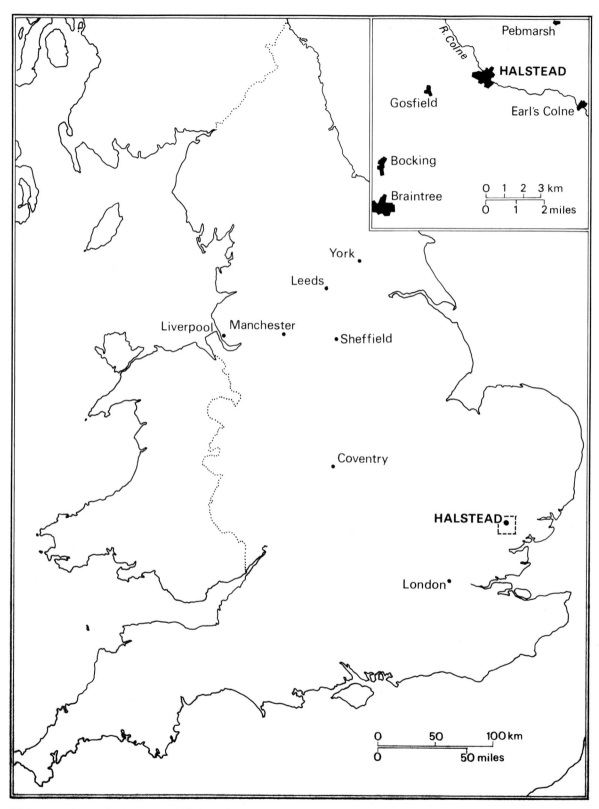

This map shows the location of Halstead

1 Introduction

In this book a case study of one firm, Samuel Courtaulds, illustrates the importance of women workers in the nineteenth-century textile industry. Although Courtaulds was a silk factory, and the majority of textile mills produced cotton or woollen cloth, it was a typical example in that women made up three quarters of the workforce. It was also typical in that the minority of men supervised the women and earned higher wages. The Courtaulds company exercised great control over the women's lives, both in and outside of the factory. In this sense too, it can be seen as representative of what happened in many textile mills. By looking in close detail at Courtaulds we can learn a great deal about the situation of women textile workers in general.

Sources

Most of the sources used come from the 1860s or thereabouts, when Samuel Courtauld's firm was at the height of its success. Many of them are documents about the way the factory was organised such as records of wages and rules kept by the company; there are original photographs of the men and women workers as well as others taken recently in Halstead; there is a map of the area. Census returns show who lived in particular houses; also included are reports by Government Investigators into housing and factory conditions, newspaper extracts and letters. The majority of quotations are from the writings of Mary Merryweather.

She was employed by Courtaulds to set up an evening school for the factory girls in 1847 and in 1862 she published a book, describing not only the school but also the women's lives. Naturally, her view is only one side of the story; for example, we have no evidence about what the factory women or men themselves actually thought, other than through Mary Merryweather's eyes, and she was from a very different background from theirs. She was also unlikely to have been too critical of her employers. However, it is unusual to have such a rich and interesting source written by a woman about women in the past.

We have included brief biographies of real people who worked in the factory from the information that is available, although their names have been changed. The purpose of these biographies is to enable readers to visualise what it might have been like to have worked at Courtaulds.

Attitudes towards women

Throughout history it has always been usual for women to work for a living. Yet it is often suggested that for women to work outside the home is a modern development. In fact, during the nineteenth century, attitudes towards women were particularly restrictive and, while their labour in factories was essential, at the same time their being there was frowned upon as unwomanly by some people.

Economic necessity forced most women, both single and married, to do whatever waged work was available. They were paid less and were more strictly disciplined than men. Meanwhile, the accepted social attitude was that they should not be out working at all, but at home fulfilling their 'womanly duties'. As the nineteenth century progressed, increasing disapproval of women working restricted their opportunities to certain jobs like textiles, where cheap labour was needed, with domestic service often as the only alternative.

Men and women in the textile industry

For many hundreds of years one of the most important industries in Britain was the spinning and weaving of cloth, both woollen and silk, which was done at home. Often the weaving was done by men, while women did the spinning – the modern word 'spinster' originally meant a women spinner.

The Industrial Revolution, which took place between about 1760 and 1830 in Britain, meant that as a result of the invention of machines, the production of textiles moved into factories. The new machines which were worked by water and steam power, were now too big to fit into the weavers' cottages. The most important textile became cotton, because it was particularly well suited to machine production, but silk was also made in the new factories.

While most textile industry was concentrated in the north of England, there were other areas like Essex, where old industries such as silk were adapted to the new conditions. In the factories men and women's jobs were once again divided, with men in the better positions; but now women were employed as both spinners and weavers. The reason given was that the new machines were lighter than the old hand looms and required less physical strength. Women and girls were also considered to be easier to discipline and therefore less trouble than men. In fact, employers were able to pay women far lower wages, since they had few alternative ways of earning. The jobs filled by men in the new factories were those of supervisors – to control the women, and mechanics – to control the machines. These jobs were regarded as 'skilled' and usually paid at least double what the women earned.

Halstead and the silk industry

One of the most important centres for the production of silk, which grew out of the Industrial Revolution and still exists as part of a major textile company today was Courtaulds mill at Halstead in Essex. In 1862 Halstead was described as:

'Very different from our northern and midland manufacturing towns. It is situated amongst the luxuriant cornfields of Essex, in the pretty valley of the Colne.'

Before the Industrial Revolution Halstead was an agricultural community with a cottage industry producing woollen cloth. Some 200-year-old weavers' cottages still standing in the town bear witness to this. When the factory system began to take over, most woollen and cotton cloth manufacture was concentrated in the north of England, and the old industries in

places like Halstead went into decline causing unemployment and poverty.

There was an old-established silk-producing centre in the south east at Spitalfields in London where, from the seventeenth century, Huguenot refugees, Protestants escaping from religious persecution in France, set up their trade. In times of trade depression, thousands of silk workers were thrown out of work and wages were cut; and as a result of rioting and industrial violence, the Spitalfields Acts of 1766 and 1773 were passed. These empowered local JP's and the Lord Mayor of London to fix weaving prices and limit the number of apprentices.

As a result, London silk merchants looked for places to establish silk mills and evade the Acts and the area around Halstead proved favourable. It was close to London, had a tradition of spinning and weaving, and a large unemployed female workforce. By about 1800 several silk firms had established mills in the area and it was as the manager of one of these mills that the first member of the Courtauld family became connected with the area.

The Courtaulds had come to England as Huguenots, but they had no link with the silk trade until George Courtauld I became an apprentice to a silk manufacturer in Spitalfields in 1775. By about 1800 he became manager of a silk-throwing mill at Pebmarsh near Halstead and in 1809 he set up a mill at Braintree; but in both cases he was employed by London firms. He later went into partnership in the Braintree business, but he was obviously not a very successful businessman. He quarrelled with his partner, dissolved the partnership and went to America where he died.

Samuel Courtauld

Courtauld's family business really began when George's son Samuel III set up business in Essex. He had worked at his father's mill at Pebmarsh and perhaps learned a good deal from his father's mistakes. In 1816 he established on his own a very small silk-throwing business at Bocking. The first few years were very hard, but by 1825 he was able to help the owner of the Town Mill in

2

Portrait of Samuel Courtauld

Halstead convert it from a corn mill to a water-powered mill, with steam installed in 1827. When the owner went bankrupt Samuel Courtauld bought the building and in 1828 the partnership of Courtauld, Taylor and Courtauld was established by deed for 21 years. The premises consisted of the wooden three-storied structure of the mill, which still stands today, with an adjoining house and garden for the mill manager and stables and coach house. By the mid nineteenth century this had grown into the largest and most successful factory in the whole country for the production of black silk mourning crape.

The silk crape industry

In Victorian England it became more and more fashionable for anyone who could afford it to go into heavy mourning, wearing black crape for at least a year after the death of a close relative. The mourner wore a dress made entirely of crape and a crape bonnet and veil, requiring yards of material. A special type of stiff silk crape was used, and by concentrating most of his production on this, Samuel Courtauld made a fortune. The demand constantly rose, there was an export market in France, and being a luxury item, profits were good. Courtauld developed a particular type of light-weight loom suitable for crape weaving, while his rival companies still used handlooms. Whereas in the 1820s there were five other silk mills in the area, by the 1850s there was only one.

Much of the success story is due to Samuel Courtauld's strong personality and drive. He was a religious man who believed in the virtues of hard work and moral standards not only for himself but for the women who worked for him. After 1849 when Samuel Courtauld and Co. was an independent company, he set up a number of social organisations for the self-improvement of his workers. He also encouraged the married women with families to work for him by providing them with facilities such as child care.

Women workers

The establishment and growth of the Halstead mill was only possible because of the large number of women who were prepared to go and work there. In the 1830s about 95% of the workers in the mill were women. By the 1870s when the numbers employed were far higher, the percentage was about 75%. At that time there was some increase in the availability of work in service according to the mill manager who recorded:

'1875 – Lost a great many workers to domestic service. A great many of our young weavers leave after they have been here from about eight to twelve months and lately most of these have gone to service there being a large demand now for domestic servants.'

For the majority of women, however, working at Courtaulds was the only opportunity for earning a wage, and even then they only received two thirds of the Spitalfields rate. For the men there was the chance of a job in one of the ironworks that made machinery, or more commonly a job in agriculture. In 1862 farm labourers in the area earned ten shillings a week; sometimes this fell to eight. This was not a living wage for a

3

Samuel Courtauld's house at Gosfield

Gravestones of the Courtauld Family

family; a quarter of this money would have gone on rent alone. Therefore a farm worker's wife was forced to work in the factory:

'The wives often told me that their husbands' wages will not buy all that is necessary; that they would rather go to the factory; that they were more fit for that work than for the harder work most cottage wives have to do'.
Mary Merryweather

As the factory prospered, so the population of Halstead grew, attracting workers from the surrounding area.

Population of Halstead 1801 3,380
1851 6,982
1861 7,500

'The labouring men, except those employed in the silk trade and other mechanical trades usually found in a small town, are agricultural labourers, drawn here in great number on account of the employment given to the women and girls of their families often to their own serious inconvenience, having to walk miles to their work'
Mary Merryweather

In 1861 one quarter of the workforce was drawn from outside Halstead, most of these being single women who lodged in the town during the week.

Courtauld's success story

During the mid nineteenth century Samuel Courtauld's company expanded steadily. Between 1835 and 1885 the firm's capital grew from £40,000 to £450,000; annual profits increased from £3,000 to £110,000. By the 1880s Courtauld had built or taken over new mills at Braintree, Chelmsford and Earl's Colne and the Halstead factory was enlarged.

In the 1850s Samuel Courtauld himself moved to an enormous country mansion at Gosfield, where he died rich and lonely in 1881. The firm however, carried on. In the 1890s Halstead was again enlarged for the production of new types of fabric like chiffon, crepon and crepe de Chine. There were now a thousand looms in operation on the site, making it one of the largest silk factories in the country. It was modernised, with telephones

installed in 1894 and electric lighting soon after. Machines that had been in operation since the 1830s were replaced with more up-to-date models.

At the end of the century there was a need for change and modernisation at Courtaulds. Heavy mourning went out of fashion so the demand for crape decreased. There was also a general depression in British industry. There were changes in the partnership, and a reorganisation of the business in an attempt to prevent profits from drastically declining. The reliance of the company on one product, which had been the key to its success at first, was now a disadvantage, and alternative products were needed.

Artificial silk

The most important step in the continuation of Courtaulds into the twentieth century was the purchase by the company in 1904 of the patents and licenses required for the exclusive British rights to use the 'viscose' process for manufacturing 'artificial silk' – now better known as rayon. This process, developed by scientists in the 1880s and 1890s, involves treating cellulose, which is obtained from wood pulp, with chemicals, which is then formed into filaments and spun into fibre or thread. Courtaulds took a risk in backing this new process and opened a factory for artificial silk production in Coventry in 1905. The Halstead mill was involved in making fabrics from the thread produced there. By the First World War rayon had replaced silk crape as Courtaulds' most profitable product.

During the 1920s the company expanded its rayon factories in various parts of Britain and abroad. They bought the exclusive rights to import rayon into the United States and set up a company there for textile production. During the Second World War they were forced to sell the American company as part of negotiations between the British and American governments for the supply of armaments to Britain. The huge amount of money now belonging to the British company, as a result, allowed for massive expansion and the take-over of other companies after the war.

The signs outside the factory, old and new

Until the recent closure of the factory, Courtaulds was one of the major employers in the town, especially for women. The old mill is still standing, but in a state of disrepair. It is hoped that one day it will be used to house a museum of the history of the company of Samuel Courtauld.

2 The workers at home

Housing

Samuel Courtauld needed a workforce for his new factory. Initially he relied upon the local population, but as his business expanded he needed to employ more workers. To encourage people to come to Halstead, he built some houses, although never enough for all his employees. The provision of a house tended to keep succeeding generations of the same family in the mill. Since most mill workers were women, keeping the home meant working for Courtauld. The majority of their husbands were employed on the land; a few in the local iron foundry. The census return shown here was fairly typical.

If you look closely at the photographs you will be able to see that the type of house the workers received depended upon the job they did in the mill. Not all the workers would have received a Courtaulds house. Some were forced to live in poorer accommodation. The larger and more imposing houses which were near the mill and had a view over the river belonged to the mechanics and overseers, who were always men. The most comfortable house, the Mill Manager's, was right next to the mill, and even had a door on the second floor leading directly to the factory. The Mill Manager was always a man. The houses further away from the mill which were smaller and less attractive were reserved for the spinners and weavers – the female workforce.

Mary Merryweather frequently visited the people of Halstead and described their houses. The houses of the weavers and spinners had three floors, with two rooms on each, one of which often housed a loom. She gives us a more detailed view of their interior.

'Not long ago I passed a night in one of these shops, a description of which would give a specimen of those belonging to the better class of our work-people. I passed through a neatly furnished parlour downstairs, into which the street door opened, then mounted stairs which led to one large room, the windows of which extended the whole of the two sides of the house, back and front. At the top of the stairs was also a very small bedroom, without any fireplace, in which the poor man I came to nurse was lying.'

Whilst she was sitting in one of the weavers' cottages, looking after the young man dying of

Number of Schedule	Road, Street and Number or Name of House	Houses		Name and Surname	Relationship to Head	Condition (Married, Single or Widowed)	Age		Rank, Profession or Occupation	Where Born	Whether Deaf, Dumb or Blind
		Inhabited	Uninhabited				Male	Female			
37	Chapel Hill	1		Isaac Payne	Head	M	40		Agricultural labourer	Halstead	
				Sarah Payne	Wife	M		35	Crape Weaver	Halstead	
				Mary Ann Payne	Daughter	S		16	Crape Winder	Halstead	
				Ann Payne	Daughter	S		14	Crape Winder	Halstead	
				James Payne	Son	S	13		Bookkeeper	Halstead	
				George Payne	Son	S	7		Scholar	Halstead	
				Robert Payne	Son	S	6		Scholar	Halstead	

1861 Census return

These houses were built near the mill by Samuel Courtauld for the Mechanics and Overseers

Mill Manager's house adjoining the factory

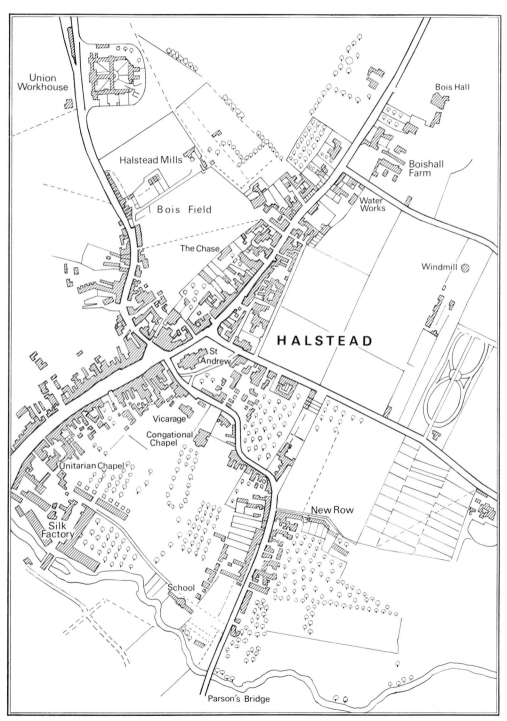

Map of Halstead

consumption, she observes and writes about the furnishing of the room, giving us an insight into their lives.

'As I sat in this room by the light of a wood and coal fire, made brighter than usual for my reception, with the addition of one dim candle, the shadows of the looms flickered strangely over the whitewashed wall and ceiling, whilst the many reminders scattered about me of the daily toil and thrift of the inmates, made me feel for the costly fabrics they contained, contrasting with the old threadbare, but well-kept greatcoat which "Father", as the good woman always called her husband, had extended on the back of the armchair to protect me from draught. On the narrow mantle-shelf were a few well worn books of family devotion, besides some of the small tools used for their work. On one side was the ticking clock, with its swinging pendulum; on the other, the little safe, or cupboard, with all the etc of their small house keepings; and around, were sundry articles of personal attire, such as you often see hung up in cottage homes. Stowed up in another part of the room were gathered seeds tied up in bundles, and other matters, telling that "Father" had an allotment garden, and worked in it, too, for the benefit of the household. On the little table beside me, were all the restoratives provided for their poor, sick son, arranged with the thoughtful care of their kind hearts, before they retired for the rest they so much needed after many nights of anxious watching. Silent and alone, the thought of the hundreds of lives which are spent almost entirely in rooms like this, came vividly before me, waking intense sympathy with them in their many trials.'

Another view of the Courtaulds housing is provided for us by the report of the 1867 Commission, which was set up by the government to look at housing conditions.

'The cottages belonging to Mr. Courtauld are, many of them newly erected and in good condition and have three bedrooms with separate entrances, and two of the three with fireplaces. Other conditions are indifferent and some miserable bad "not fit for human habitation" and in the opinion of Dr. Borham, who is acquainted with them, a prolific source of rheumatism followed in many cases by consumption.'

The members of the Commission felt that the new houses were quite suitable, but were less impressed by the older ones, which according to Dr. Borham were a source of disease.

The commission also recorded the rent paid by the workers:

'The rent of the new cottages is from 1s.4d. to 1s.9d. with from 16 to 25 roods which let at from 4d. to 6d. per rood according to the quality of the land...'

Many of Samuel Courtauld's houses are still standing. The weavers' cottages built in 1872 were show pieces. They had both gas and running water.

Weavers' Cottages built before Samuel Courtauld's time

Home life

Despite the luxury of gas and running water for some tenants, life for most of the women was hard. Not only did they have to work in the factories six days a week, but they were also responsible for looking after the home and family. Sunday, their only day off from the mill, which should have been a day of rest, and probably was for the men, was the only time the women could catch up on their household chores.

'Sunday morning is the time of general tidying up, and cooking a bit of meat dinner, which usually cost threepence [3d] or fourpence [4d] per lb. fried or stewed, and a few potatoes. The working clothes are mended, patched, or washed, ready for Monday morning'.

Mary Merryweather

Many women, as well as working in the mill full-time and caring for their homes and families, had the additional responsibility of a lodger from Monday to Saturday. The lodgers tended to live in the outlying villages. They would walk into Halstead on Mondays, lodge with a family, and return to their homes on Saturday after work. Samuel Courtauld actively encouraged his tenants to take in lodgers. He provided beds free and paid their board and lodging of 1s a week. Some of Samuel Courtauld's workers only received a house on the condition that they took in a lodger.

In many of the homes an interesting arrangement occurred. Before Samuel Courtauld had weaving machines in his factory, this process was carried out in the

Weavers' Cottages built by Samuel Courtauld

home, most frequently by the husbands of the women who worked in the mill. The looms were kept in the two rooms on the middle floor. Miss Merryweather gives us an idea of a typical scene in a weaver's house during the day. It shows that weavers frequently coupled their job with keeping an eye on the children, the elder of whom cared for the younger until their mother came home from work.

'A weavers shop must usually be both his kitchen and his sitting-room, because he cannot afford a fire elsewhere, as well as a sufficient one there – warmth being very necessary for his work; and neither frequent cleaning, nor thorough ventilation, are very possible when delicate and expensive work is in the loom. Thus neatness and health often suffer. In such shops are often to be seen the men sitting in the click-clacking loom, with half-a-dozen children toddling or trotting in and out. Sometimes one of these would creep away, and shyly hide her face behind the large, rough stones, tied to the end of the harness to keep it steady; sometimes a baby face would peep out of a high wicker cradle, the infant lost in what looked like dirty rags; whilst sitting on a tiny stool, or kneeling at the side of the cradle, might be seen another little one, scarcely larger than the baby, but taught to rock it till mother came from the factory.'

The extract suggests that it was a fairly passive eye that the men kept on their children, and anything they needed doing was done by the mother when she returned from work.

Many of the women working at Courtaulds must have suffered under the strain of having two full-time occupations – a job at the mill which often supplied the family with a home, and caring for this house and family.

3 The workers at the factory

Halstead Mill

Halstead Mill was first used for grinding corn into flour. It was converted to a silk mill in 1825 by Samuel Courtauld. The mill was originally built on the River Colne because water was needed to power the machines. Steam was introduced in 1827 because the water power from the river was not sufficiently strong for the new machinery.

The factory was built of timber on three floors. Mary Merryweather describes what it was like inside the mill:

'The impression on my mind of my first entrance there is still very deep and lively. At one glance from the door of the basement floor of a large brick building, I could see 500 looms at work by steam-power with a women tending each. It was a clean, airy, and well-arranged factory, though to a newcomer it seemed very confusing, with its click-clacking of machinery and the great swift bands which kept all going; almost suspending thought by their manifestation of impelling power. Above this large room were two floors partly devoted also to the weaving of gauze for crape, and partly to the other processes of winding.'

Making silk

Raw silk produced by silk worms came mainly from Italy. It was spun on machines similar to the ones in the picture on page 14. This process was called winding. The spun silk was then woven into cloth on the loom. Some of the silk was then crimped, which meant that it was pleated. Only men were allowed to work the crimping machine. It was considered a highly secret operation and crimpers had to swear an oath of secrecy to a Justice of the Peace up until the First World War. Women were not even allowed into the room.

Selling silk

This material was made up into dresses and sold in shops like Peter Robinson, who had a whole store devoted to mourning clothes. Clothes and rules for mourning were advertised in ladies magazines. Even in royal circles mourning was strictly observed. Queen Victoria thought even young babies should be dressed in black if a relative died. In 1859 she wrote to her daughter whose mother-in-law had just died:

'I think it quite wrong that the nursery are not in mourning.'

When the Princess Beatrice was only three she dressed her in mourning and stated:

'Darling Beatrice looks lovely in her black silk and crape dress.'

The secret crimping machine for pleating the silk

Halstead Mill

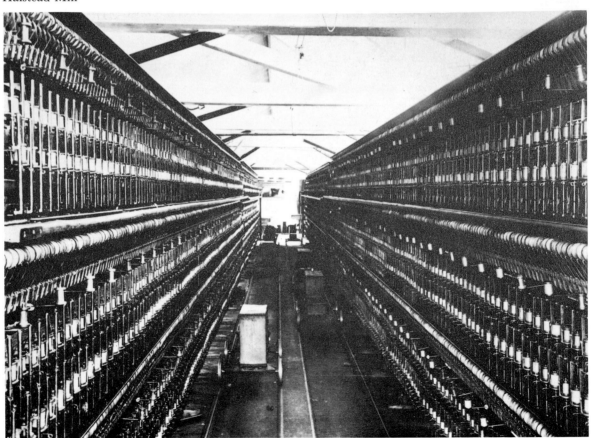

A winding machine

A loom for weaving silk

Jobs and wages

In 1861 there were about 901 females and 114 males working in Courtauld's factory. Although there were fewer men, they all either worked in the offices or were mechanics or overseers. Women were the ones who actually made the silk.

'No man would like to work a power loom, there is such a clattering and noise it would almost make some men mad.'

Select Committee on Hand Loom Weavers' Petitions, 1834

Winding was the job of young boys until the age of 15 and young girls up to the age of 17. Winding was not considered suitable work for a man, so most boys left the mill, perhaps to become agricultural labourers, or to work in some small trade in the town, such as shoe-making. Only a few stayed on at the mill to become mechanics or overseers. The girls

A piece of mourning crape

FAMILY MOURNING.

Messrs. JAY

would respectfully announce that great economy is effected by purchasing Mourning at their Establishment, 247 and 249, REGENT STREET.

THEIR STOCK OF FAMILY MOURNING

being the largest in Europe.

Though Messrs. Jay professedly keep the best articles for Mourning and Half-Mourning—at all times the cheapest—they supply a Complete Suit of Domestic Mourning for 2½ guineas.

MOURNING COSTUME

of every description is kept Ready Made, and can be forwarded in Town or Country at a moment's notice.

The most reasonable prices are charged, and the wear of every article is guaranteed.

THE LONDON GENERAL

MOURNING WAREHOUSE,

REGENT STREET,

(next the Circus),

JAYS'.

An advertisement for family mourning clothes from the 1870s

15

however usually remained at Courtaulds, transferring from the spinning section of the factory to the more skilled task of weaving.

The only time both men and women did the same work was in old age, when workers of both sexes were put on to cleaning and packing work. Even then men and women were treated differently; some men were given an allowance of between 3s and 4s a week when they retired, whereas most women received no money at all.

In the 1860s if workers arrived more than five minutes late they found the entrance gate to the factory closed. The foreman then had to grant them permission to enter. However, if this happened too many times the workers would be sent home and lose a half-day's pay.

Most factories at this time had rules and regulations which all workers had to obey. Fines were often imposed if people disobeyed these rules. A typical set of rules found in a factory would be:

Any spinner found with window open	1s
Any spinner found dirty at work	1s
Any spinner found whistling	1s
Any spinner found talking	1s
Any spinner found singing	1s

This may not seem much money to us but it was quite a large sum out of a small wage of 10s a week.

Workers were fined if the silk was of an inferior quality. These fines were still in force as late as 1908. Weavers were fined between 1d and 3d for dirty or uneven cloth.

Women often licked the full bobbins of silk to smooth down the ends of the thread but Samuel Courtauld forbade this in 1860. He suspected the women of trying to make the bobbins heavier in order to increase their wages. Women were fined between $\frac{1}{4}$d and 1d if they were caught licking bobbins.

Courtauld did not just expect good work from his employees; he also wished to influence their characters. Painted on the walls were the words:

'Weave truth with trust,
Honour to whom honour is due'.

Women in mourning dress

16

EMPLOYMENT OF
LITTLE BOYS
AT THE
SILK FACTORIES.

BOYS will now be taken to the Silk-winding, at the Bocking Factory, between the ages of Twelve and Thirteen-and-a-half.

BUT at Fifteen years of age, these boys will have to leave the Silk mills, and seek other employment.

BECAUSE there is not in the Mills fitting employment for any considerable number of grown-up Men, and because it therefore would not be for the ultimate advantage of Boys to be allowed to remain at such work as Silk-winding after Fifteen years of age.

SAMUEL COURTAULD & Co.

Sept. 13th, 1859.

A. CARTER, PRINTER AND BINDER, HALSTEAD.

A factory notice about the employment of boys

The Courtauld workforce in 1861

	Number	Approximate weekly wages	Most frequent Age	Marital status
Mill Manager	1	£1,000 per annum (+ 3% profits)	over 30	married
Overseers and clerks	26	15s–32s 6d	over 30	married
Mechanics and engine drivers	6	17s–25s 6d	over 30	married
Carpenters and blacksmiths	3	14s–21s	over 30	married
Lodgekeeper (who also did soft silk weaving at home)	1	15s + handloom produce	over 40	married
Power loom machinery attendants and steamers	16	14s–15s	over 20	married
Mill machinery attendants and loom cleaners	18	10s–15s	over 20	married
Spindle cleaners, bobbin stampers and packers, messengers, sweepers	5	5s–12s	14–25, over 40	single and married
Watchmen	—	7s–10s	—	—
Coachmen, grooms and van driver	—	5s–10s	—	—
Winders	38	2s–4s 6d	12–15	single
Total males	114			
Gauze examiners	4	10s–11s	over 30	married
Female assistant overseers	4	9s–10s	over 30	married
Warpers	16	7s 6d–10s	over 20	married
Twisters	9	7s–10s	over 20	married
Wasters	4	6s 6d–9s	over 20	married
Weavers	589	5s 6d–8s	over 17	married and single
Plugwinders	2	6s–7s 6d	over 20	married
Drawers and doublers	83	4s 6d–6s 6d	over 17	married
Winders	188	2s–4s 6d	12–17	single
Housekeeper	1	—	—	—
Schoolteacher	1	—	—	—
Total females	901			
Grand total males and females	1,015			

TRUCK ACT, 1896.

REGISTER OF DEDUCTIONS AND PAYMENTS.

No. of Case.	Date.	Name.	Nature of the Act or Omission.	Amount.
13	May 22nd 1908	Rose Sparrow	Gally + thin places	3d
14	June 12th 1908	Edith Willsher	Thick + thin places	3d
15	June 26th 1908	Florence Carter	Dirty. Thick + thin places +2 holes	3d
16	July 3rd 1908	Eliza Goodey	A float 2 ins Double Ended shoot + thick + thin places	1/-
17	July 10th 1908	Ada Burst	Gally. A Hole + thin places	3d
18	Sept 18th 1908	Jessie Scillitoe	Thick + thin places. Threads run out A float. Dirty + Bad Leisure	3d

Fines in the factory

The rules about dress only applied to the women who were encouraged to look clean and decent. Despite his efforts, however, some women did not change their ways.

'The women were generally clean and tidily dressed; but some were, in spite of the pains taken by the overseers about it, very dirty and ill-dressed.'
Mary Merryweather

In October 1860 a rule was introduced forbidding the wearing of hoops or crinolines because they were thought to be dangerous, as well as indecent if the wearer stood above floor level. Some women felt that it gave more freedom to their legs and reduced the burden of petticoats.

Other factories similarly forbade women to wear crinolines because of the risk of accidents.

DRESS.

OCTOBER 9th, 1860.

IT is always a pleasure to us to see our workpeople, and especially our comely young women, dressed NEAT and TIDY; nor should we, as has been already declared in a notice that has been put up at Bocking Mills, wish to interfere with the fashion of their dress, whatever it may be, so long as their dress does not interfere with their work, or with the work of those near them in our employ.

The present ugly fashion of HOOPS, or CRINOLINE, as it is called, is, however, quite unfitted for the work of our Factories. Among the Power Looms it is almost impossible, and highly dangerous; among the Winding and Drawing Engines it greatly impedes the free passage of Overseers, Wasters, &c., and is inconvenient to all. At the Mills it is equally inconvenient, and still more mischievous, by bringing the dress against the Spindles, while also it sometimes becomes shockingly indecent when the young people are standing upon the Sliders.

FOR ALL THESE REASONS

We now request all our Hands, at all our Factories, to leave HOOPS AND CRINOLINE at home when they come to the Factories to work; and to come dressed in a manner suitable for their work, and with as much BECOMING NEATNESS as they can.

And OVERSEERS at all the Floors are hereby charged to see that all the Hands coming to work are thus properly dressed for factory work—without Hoops or Crinoline of any sort; and Overseers will be held RESPONSIBLE to us for strict regard to this regulation.

Rules about dress

Licking Bobbins.

WHEN a Bobbin is fastened off, it has been a common practice to touch the end with the tongue to smooth it down, and there is no harm in that.

But out of this practice has arisen another practice, both nasty and mischievous, of licking the Bobbins all over to make them weigh heavier.

And to put an end at once, and altogether, to this nasty and mischievous practice of Licking the Bobbins, we now make it

A RULE

Not to touch the Bobbins with the Tongue at all; and Overseers are hereby authorised to enforce this rule by Forfeits.

SAMUEL COURTAULD & Co.

A rather unusual factory rule

18

'We have not had any fatal or serious accidents here, the loss of a finger or so. But there have been several losses of crinolines and dresses from being caught in the shafts...It is a very awkward thing for the girl sets up a great screaming, and all the rest do the same. I have known three caught in one day, and then perhaps a month without any. Finding that some check was necessary, I put a fine for it and no one was caught for three months afterwards. It might be thought, as was indeed said to me, that the fright and the loss of the dress were punishment enough, but it is clear that the fine was wanted.'
Mr George Boyce, Manager, Children's Employment Commission, 3rd Report, 1864

One particular woman, Matilda Davies, lost her life as a result of wearing a large crinoline.

'Matilda Davies had lived with us as a lodger...and had worked at two factories before she lost her life and had been caught several times in the machinery...and one of the times the skirt of her dress was ripped off...she was a strong, but not a careful young woman, and wore a very large crinoline, which I think was a great deal the cause of her accident.'
Louisa Leake, Children's Employment Commission, 3rd Report, 1864.

Food and drink

Some women lived a long way from the factory and could not go home at lunch time. There was no canteen at the Halstead Mill but workers were allowed to heat up their food, boil potatoes and make tea. In winter soup was sold for $\frac{1}{4}$d a pint, and dumplings for $\frac{1}{2}$d.

'The kitchen was needed not only to provide suitable cooking for the sick, but as an accommodation for those working in the factory, who came from the distant villages, and who breakfasted and dined in it. It possessed a good range, with oven and boiler. A copper was fixed in one corner for the purpose of making soup. Leading out of the kitchen was a scullery and a pantry, with a sliding shutter and a dresser in it, from which to dispense the viands given away. Soup was made from Soyer's recipe twice a week in winter and sold at $\frac{1}{4}$d a pint. Flour and suet dumplings were boiled in the soup, and sold for one half-penny [$\frac{1}{2}$d] each; thus our factory women could, on those days at least, if they brought their bread with them have a comfortable dinner for three halfpence [$1\frac{1}{2}$d].

This notice tells us about cooking lunch at the factory

Mothers who had no possibility of cooking at home, could, when they left the factory, take home something for their own and their children's dinners. A good fire for the women at meal times, and tea made for them at cost price at breakfast, render the kitchen a most valuable establishment. It is not at present large enough for those who would gladly avail themselves of its accommodation and it is hoped a larder may before long be provided.'   *Mary Merryweather*

The kitchen was only open on the condition that the women behaved properly and used it well. It was a privilege and not a right.

'The conduct of these people in the kitchen some time ago was such as made me doubt if we must not close the kitchen to them at meal times; but on certain measures of reform being taken, coupled with a threatening to report delinquents, it was found unnecessary; and from the gradual better condition of the whole factory population, I believe their conduct is at present orderly, and their gratitude for the accommodation frequently expressed.'
Mary Merryweather

Some benefits however were reserved for male employees. Beer allowances were common in factories throughout the nineteenth century and in Courtaulds beer was given to men involved in dirty work.

'It has hitherto been the procedure of the firm to make an allowance of beer to such of their hands as have had any extraordinary hard or dirty work to do. These allowances have hitherto and will continue to be made at the discretion and judgement of the Manager and he is strictly required not to make any such allowance in any case whatever except he shall conscientiously believe the job for which the allowance is made is that of exceptional character, the quantity of beer allowed is two pints per day, one at 11 a.m. and one at 4 p.m.   *Bocking factory rules*

Making money

The pattern of women's work was different from that of men. Men worked continuously throughout their life and progressed slowly up the hierarchy. Women however had a broken work pattern because of the time they took off to have children. Nevertheless even if women remained single they tended to remain in the lowliest positions. It was the cheap labour of the mill women which enabled Samuel Courtauld to make his profits; he made further profits out of women from the wealthier classes to whom he sold mourning clothes.

These are some of Samuel Courtauld's mill workers

These are some of Samuel Courtauld's mechanics

MALE	FEMALE
1 Winder	1 Winder
2 Messenger (or spindle cleaner, bobbin stamper, packer or sweeper)	2 Weaver (or plugwinder, drawer, waster or assistant overseer in winding)
3 Power loom attendant or mill machinery attendant (or steamer or loom cleaner)	3 Warper (or twister or gauze examiner)
4 Overseer or clerk (or mechanic or engine driver)	

If they lived to old age, then some men would go back to (2) above.

Some men were put on the firm's 'allowance list' when they were too old to work or no longer needed.

If they lived to old age, then some women were put on sweeping or other jobs under (2) in the male hierarchy.

There is no record of any women on the 'allowance list' after they left.

This diagram shows the different work patterns of men and women

4 The workers' social life

A fatherly influence

The influence Samuel Courtauld had over the women workers extended far beyond the hours they spent in the mill. He acted rather like a father figure, guiding and controlling their private lives as well. He was the type of employer, fairly typical of Victorian England, who is often described as 'paternalistic'. He believed it was his duty to exert a good influence over his employees and to encourage them to improve themselves. This applied especially to the women, from whom a higher standard of behaviour and morality was expected than from the men. Also, because the women were responsible for running the home and bringing up children, it was in the firm's interest to provide them with facilities such as a nursery. This enabled the women to do two jobs – as factory workers and as wives and mothers.

Samuel Courtauld did not try to improve the material well-being of the women by increasing their wages; the wages he paid were extremely low. Neither did he believe in providing them with the facilities and letting them organise things for themselves. Everything done for the women was controlled by the company, as the company thought best. This is how Mary Merryweather described Courtauld's policy:

'It was explained to me that although the rate of wages, according to the rules of social economy, could not be advanced, yet nothing prevented them from bettering the condition of their work people by providing educational and other ameliorations of their condition. The practice of unrestricted almsgiving was discussed as undesirable, except in cases of illness, and this from its invariable tendency to destroy all healthy self dependence and energy.'

During the 1850s and 1860s Samuel Courtauld and his wife organised a school, adult education classes, a library and institute, nursery, mother's club, sick fund, amusement society, and lodging house – all with the aim of improving the character of the women who attended. Apart from the literary institute, all these schemes were for women rather than men. There were other organisations for the men such as a Temperance Society and a Penny Bank.

The Courtaulds also got information from the supervisors in the mill about the women's behaviour outside work. A woman whose behaviour did not meet with approval lost her job. This particularly applied to relationships with men. According to the Mill Manager's diary, in 1871, a single woman weaver called Eliza Harrington was 'dismissed for living with a man unmarried'. In 1884 Hannah Cooper of Tidings Hill was dismissed for 'having an illegitimate child'. Having one illegitimate child was normally allowed, but to have a second meant dismissal. In 1850 a weaver called Sarah Payne lost her job for 'helping a girl to procure an abortion'. In 1888 the case of Mrs Beckwith took up a whole page in the Mill Manager's diary.

'A young widow named Beckwith living at the yard who received all sorts of men at her house, especially Henry Bowles, from the mills. Mr Courtauld told me we cannot employ such women and must dismiss them'.

Men might be dismissed for fighting or drunkeness, but not for their relationships with women.

Visible signs

Because Samuel Courtauld tried to organise so much of the women's lives for them, he very much made his mark on Halstead, and this is still in evidence today. As early as 1846 the partners provided entertainments for the workforce, but in that year some of the senior male employees decided to reverse the procedure; they put on a dinner in a marquee attended by fifteen hundred mill workers and their employers. These senior employees obviously valued Courtauld's good opinion:

'The fete...from which the work people – who were almost all in the employ of one firm of silk manufacturers – had met to give an entertainment to their employers, and to present to them several beautiful silk banners with mottoes and devices expressive of the good feeling existing between them and their masters, together with an emblematic medal designed and struck for the occasion.'

Mary Merryweather

The medals had the Courtaulds' mottoes on them which can still be seen written up in large letters inside the factory.

Many of the houses still standing were built by Courtaulds for the workforce; as well as the hospital and the Homes of Rest, built for the elderly in the 1920s. The school in which Mary Merryweather taught was not demolished until 1980. The coffee rooms, built by Courtaulds in the late nineteenth century still stand; also the Public Gardens which were funded by a £1,000 donation from the company. In 1887, to mark Queen Victoria's Golden Jubilee, an imposing water fountain was presented to the town by George Courtauld, Samuel's nephew. It still stands at the top of Market Hill. The modern factory was built in the 1920s next to the old mill on the river, and the initials SAC can be seen on many of the buildings near here.

This water fountain was presented to the town by Samuel Courtauld's nephew

The die for this medal was presented to Samuel Courtauld by some of his workers in 1846. The factory mottoes are written on it.

Today Halstead is a busy town with a variety of employment, while many of its inhabitants travel to work elsewhere. Still, however, many older people can remember the days before the last war when the Courtaulds mill was the only place for women to find work. Families still live in the weavers' cottages and many people have stories to tell about the firm and its involvement with the town. In Halstead in the 1980s Samuel Courtauld is still a household name, and the influence of the man who first came here 150 years ago can still be felt.

Education

Mary Merryweather was employed by the Courtaulds to set up a school for the factory girls in 1847. This is how she described her appointment:

'The wife of the senior partner had been wishing to do more in the way of education and kindly oversight for the working people of their larger factory, which was at the town of Halstead; and they were still looking out for some lady who would undertake to read and lecture to the factory girls, who, now that the Ten Hours Bill [restricting employment of women and children to ten hours per day] had come into operation, had much more time at their command without much wisdom as to how to employ it'.

She found that most young girls working in the factory had little education. Although there were three schools in the town there was, as yet, no compulsory state education, and girls from an early age got jobs looking after the factory women's babies.

'A great many of the young people in the factory had, however, been to none of these, having learned to read, but imperfectly at the Sunday school: or if they had been at the day school it was rarely that they had remained there after they were old enough to nurse a baby; it might be the mother's or some other woman's who worked in the factory and would pay 1s 6d per week, which was quite sufficient inducement for most parents to take the poor girl from her school'

Mary Merryweather opened an evening school for girls. It was free, and attracted some unruly pupils:

These are 'homes of rest' built for the elderly Courtauld workers in the early 1920s

24

'In a few weeks we met in the Girls British School room; about 120 entered the first week. Our first school-nights were unsettling and exciting. A great many of the most disorderly girls were attracted by the novelty; they would come and see what this new teacher was like, and have some fun as they thought...It would have made it much easier to manage at first if all the weavers above seventeen had been made to pay at least a penny a week: it being free, there was great crowding and crushing up to be classified. Some of those who came were coarse, noisy girls, with no womanly reserve or modesty; they pushed, jested and even swore at each other'.

Discipline was by no means easy:

'The noisy groups of rough factory girls used to yell or scream as they came or went in a way to cause me constant alarms. It was found quite necessary to find some means to check it; so one girl, who was more disorderly than the rest, was discharged from her work at the factory for a while. This had the wished-for effect'.

Mary Merryweather taught the girls the basic subjects, but as she explained, part of the purpose of the school was to change the girls attitudes and habits:

'The evening school was the sphere in which I felt that most hope lay – if that were attractive, the young girls would have a retreat from that which was coarse and depraving, either in their homes, lodgings and other haunts.'

From among the better pupils she appointed monitors whose job it was to supervise and help teach the others. This is a letter written to her by one of the monitors a few months after the school opened.

May 21st 1848

Dear Lady,

With unspeakable pleasure I recieved your kind little note; I think it a great favour to all of us to be allowed to write to you, as I'm sure I do improve in my writing; I feel that it is my duty to try to assist you in the school in every way I can. I often wonder how you can look so pleased when there is such a confusion in the school. For I know that you take a great many pains to instruct us, and still there are some that do not behave themselves as they ought to, but we will try to turn them by kind words if we can...

Believe me to remain,
Your obedient scholar,

HB

Another letter, written by Mrs Courtauld, was complimentary about the girls' good behaviour:

'On the factory fete day, at Folly House, I could have counted out your girls from Halstead by their quiet, enjoying, respectable behaviour. This is very encouraging and delightful. Labour is never thrown away, so we must work away'.

Mary Merryweather found that the best pupils were those from homes where their parents encouraged them to educate themselves, rather than those who lived independently in lodgings, who had less respect for education:

'It may be as well to mention that those girls who lived in lodgings were seldom the most constant at attendants of the evening school, as we might have expected they should be, having fewer duties to engage them at home. Those most constantly at school were invariably those whose homes were decent, and whose parents were conscious of the advantages to be derived from the school, and therefore sent them even at a sacrifice to themselves. Still, very many good girls found it impossible always to come away from domestic duties; and when I knew such was the real cause of detention, I always encouraged their serving the home affections first'.

Child care

About a third of the women in the mill were married and Courtaulds tried to take over their arrangements for child care. Mary Merryweather described the usual situation, which was that a mother paid a young girl to look after her baby if there was no-one else at home.

'Few results of our factory life impressed me more painfully, when I first mixed with the inhabitants of Halstead, than the neglect of infants, whose mothers worked at the factory. A poor woman, as soon as she could leave her house after the child was born, usually found some little girl to attend to the child, if her husband worked at home and she had no elder children of her own. Sometimes however, she took the poor baby, on her way to the factory at six o'clock in the morning, to a neighbour's house probably an old woman who took charge of several others. It was not wonderful if, with either of the these plans, the infants were badly off. Even the mothers themselves not

25

unfrequently (supposing their babies would be safer in the cradles than in the arms of their tiny or careless mothers) gave them sleeping doses, and by this means often, no doubt, brought their children into what they term 'decline' – a wasting away, which would in all probability have been prevented if the commonest rules of health and good nursing had been attended to.'

Mary Merryweather

Mrs Courtauld was responsible for setting up a nursery for the children of the mill women:

'It was agreed that a room at the Home should be appropriated to an Infant Nursery. This was opened in December 1850, and we continued it until September 1853. We commenced with six cradles, and the first week received three babies.'

These were the rules for the nursery.

1 No child will be admitted unless it has been vaccinated and is in a state of health.

2 Children will be received at any age between one month and two years.

3 Fourpence[4d] a day will be charged for the care and food of each child; and it is required that the money be brought with the child each morning, otherwise, the nurse has strict orders to refuse admission.

4 The child's clothing must be perfectly clean. All extra linen is provided by the nursery.

5 Unweaned children may be nursed at the Institution by their mothers during the day.

Not only were there rules, but the way in which the children were treated was quite different from what their mothers thought was the right way. Mary Merryweather describes the kinds of issues that led to conflict:

'At first I was in the nursery to help wash the little ones, knowing what a strong objection some of our people had to the children being washed all over; particularly the poor little head, which, in some cases, was in a very sad condition before it came, for want of care. The mothers were encouraged to stay and assist when their work permitted, and in this way some education in the common sense of infant management went on; their notions of stuffing very young children with unlikely food had to be dealt with; and our plan of only giving milk and water or milk and bread and sometimes arrowroot, was thought very insufficient'

The nursery was one of the Courtauld schemes that failed, and it closed in less than three years, because the women refused to use it.

'Fifteen babies were the greatest number we ever had on the books as brought at one time to the nursery, and then we had four nurses – two elderly women and two girls under them. As it was – partly owing to a very severe spring in 1853, and the prevalence of bronchitis among the infants; partly to the extra trouble the mothers had in bringing the children to us, instead of having them fetched as other nurses would do; besides the convenience of having little maids at home to light the fire, boil their kettle, or look after other children – the attendance at the nursery diminished. It was disappointing after all our pains and care...'

Another way of influencing the mothers was through the monthly Mothers' Meetings which were started in 1850 by Mrs Clements, the vicar's wife. There were readings from books, discussions, tea parties, but also instruction on good motherhood:

'The President has uniformly impressed on the minds of the mothers, as the best means of domestic government, the law of kindness, commenting on the bad effects of harsh treatment, scolding and violent language sometimes addressed to children among the poor. She has urged quietness of manner as the most efficient and useful in gaining the affectionate obedience of children'

Mary Merryweather

Health and cleanliness

The most common occurrence of illness in Halstead was among those who lived in the poorer houses near the river, which were damp and frequently flooded. Mary Merryweather often visited the sick and here she described the state of health of the town:

'Consumption is our most frequent complaint; and it would be impossible for me to recollect the great number I have visited who have died of it after long months, sometimes years of sickness. Low fever is seldom absent from the cottages near the river, and almost every autumn, typhus appears: Besides the fever we have twice in ten years had smallpox in the town, owing, in

Samuel Courtauld's initials can still be seen in many places in Halstead today

some degree, no doubt, to the neglect of vaccination, as so many of the poor have a strong conviction that other diseases and taints of the blood are often conveyed to their children through that means.'

Also, working conditions in the mill caused health problems among the women.

'The warmth also, in which they find it most easy to work the silk, has a great tendency to make them sensitive to cold in various forms; for the young growing girls it is highly disadvantageous to their health in many ways, as it adds to their precocity of mind and body.'

There was no hospital and very few nurses in the town at this time:

'The want of nurses was very great, especially amongst the poor. Those decent women who might have become nurses, were deterred by the fears of themselves or families from entering an infected house, and refused to do so even when offered payment that would have been tempting under other circumstances.'

During epidemics Mrs Courtauld would sometimes send to London for nurses. The main source of medical treatment seems to have been the doctor, and a doctor's club was organised by Courtaulds so that the women could pay regularly for treatment when needed. However, there was some dissatisfaction with the scheme.

'At that time there was, as there still is, a doctor's club at the factory. Most of the women pay one penny [1d] a week to it, enabling them to have advice and medicine in sickness. This is a great comfort, and if they go to the doctor in time, and if they have proper care and attention at the dispensary, it is a capital plan; but with us I cannot say it has been perfectly satisfactory to the greater number. I do not know with how much reason, but there was a prevalent feeling that many of the necessary medicines being too expensive were never given to the members of the club.'

The hospital built by Samuel Courtauld in 1884 and which is still in use today

28

Mary Merryweather noticed that women's health often suffered more than men's because they were less likely to belong to an insurance scheme, and so could not afford to take time off from work.

'Illness of a very serious nature is the result of inattention to the…symptoms, and this with working women more frequently than with men; perhaps because they more seldom belong to provident sick clubs, and therefore are less willing to forego their earnings.'

In 1857 a sickness club was organised for the women by the factory manager. Courtaulds contribution was to donate the money they had confiscated in fines from the women.

'Every member of the club pays one penny a week to this fund, which entitles her to a relief in sickness adjusted according to the income of the club, but amounting to about 3s 6d or 4s a week, for twelve weeks, and then half the amount for twelve weeks more. Of course a medical certificate is required each week.'

The club was managed by a committee of six women from the factory. Some of these became involved in an evening class on medicine.

'Four out of the six young women on the committee formed a little class with me on Monday evenings for the purpose of reading, learning and considering subjects relating to sickness, and the means within the reach of most women for amelioration or prevention.'

Other attempts were made to influence the women's attitudes towards health, and particularly cleanliness. For example, in the school:

'The admonition to wash all over each day was received by many as a most absurd and impossible thing; one blunt girl declaring she did not believe she had been in a bath since she was a baby!'

And in the Mothers' Meetings:

'Special attention has been paid to urge on mothers the importance of cleanliness and order; but great difficulties are experienced in these matters, as the uniform reply of Factory mothers is, that they have no time for these things.'

Later, in 1884, Courtaulds founded a hospital for the people of Halstead. While the firm provided the building, the local community had to find all the furnishings and fittings. The hospital is still in use today, as a small cottage hospital. Many of the patients are old and have worked for Courtaulds in the past.

The lodging house

Single women who worked at the factory took lodgings in the town, and taking in a lodger was an extra source of income for many a poor family. Courtaulds, anxious to influence the morals of these girls for the better, opened a lodging house where they could stay. Mary Merryweather explained the reasons:

'In November, 1849, was opened by the Messrs Courtauld, a Factory Home, for the benefit of our unmarried work-women of good character. The reasons may be easily imagined by all who have any knowledge of the morals of a factory population. The evils resulting from the bad accommodation in the ordinary over-crowded cottages, and in the common lodging-houses, came fearfully before us. Many young and very ignorant girls were, for the sake of work, brought from rural districts; away from home and parents, without restraint from within or without, sometimes even the worst of examples in the house which their penury, or want of experience, tempted them to accept as their temporary home. At that time a class of women particularly adverse to morality were among those who received these young girls into their houses, and positively helped to instruct and encourage them in abandoned courses. Many such women were at work in the factory, and have been since expelled. Facts, far too sad and shocking for me to write, frequently came to light.'

However, there was opposition to the plan from the townspeople:

'The majority of the poor townspeople, however, opposed our plan in their own circles very strongly; some from interested motives, thinking they should by it lose their lodgers, whose money helped to pay their rent; whilst others, from the love of unrestricted liberty, (as they conceive it,) did all they could to set the girls against it, circulating reports which were too ridiculous to have been believed, one would have thought, by any but the most ignorant.'

Mary Merryweather described the house, where she too lived.

'It was a large pleasant airy dwelling, with spacious offices, flower and kitchen gardens. We began by engaging a strong middle aged servant who was called 'housekeeper'. She had a sitting room near the entrance door, and opposite the door of the long kitchen, or, dining hall of the young women; they had another large room in the house, which was used on Sundays or when they pleased as their sitting room; there were eight bedrooms, with from two to five single beds in each.'

It cost 1s a week for board, lodging, and washing, plus 2d a week to be kept to pay for lodging in case of illness. These were the rules:

1 The home is to be open from half-past five o'clock in the morning till nine, winter, and ten summer evenings.

2 The gas in the bedrooms to be put out not later than a quarter past ten.

3 Each lodger to make her own bed before nine in the morning; and those in one room to take turns each week to clean out their bedrooms.

4 No lodger to remain in her bedroom after nine in the morning, or to return to it before eight in the evening, without permission of the superintendent.

5 Each lodger will have a small cupboard to herself, the key of which will be given her on her entrance, and returned by her on leaving the Home. All property belonging to lodgers will be considered as under their own care, and at their own risk.

6 Each lodger will be provided with a tray, two plates, two basins, a jug, a teapot, a cup and saucer, a knife and fork, and two spoons, which will be under her own care; and on her leaving the Home they are to be returned to the superintendent in a sound state.

7 The property of the establishment is to be treated with due care; and in particular, no cutting or writing on tables, forms, chairs, or windows etc.; no defacing the walls to be permitted: any damage done by a lodger to be made good at her expense.

8 Modest and gentle manners, decent and becoming language, and habits of cleanliness, are expected in all the lodgers, and no one guilty of misconducting herself in these respects will be permitted to remain in the Home.

The girls obviously did not like the rules, they often rebelled against them and eventually burned them.

'Indeed for the first few years it would be difficult to describe the strong aversion the lodgers generally expressed to having any rules referred to; they almost resented it as an insult, and several times, notwithstanding the arguments frequently used with them to show that the general good demanded some such regulations, have the copies of the rules been taken from different rooms in the house and burnt by the girls.'

During the 1850s there were, on average only 15 girls in the home at one time. Altogether during the first seven years, 67 girls stayed for some time at the home. Eventually, however, it closed, because so few girls would live there. Like the nursery, this was one of Samuel Courtauld's less successful schemes.

Mary Merryweather described some of the girls who stayed there:

'Anything like work out of the factory was the exception, not the rule. The lesser respectable amongst them were very lazy and would sit hours in the evening without anything to do, or else idle about the town...some really did not seem able to make a bed, or do anything tidily in the house when they first came.'

Leisure

A number of attempts were made by Courtaulds to influence how the women spent their leisure time. Mary Merryweather disapproved strongly of the common pastime of going to the pub:

'I soon became aware of many and sad immoralities, especially the very common habit of frequenting the public-houses; not only did the men congregate there but many women also, wasting their time, and money, and enticing others comparatively innocent in to their shameful ways. Frequently the evening attraction was a penny dance, accompanied of course with immoderate drinking and low songs.'

Mr and Mrs Courtauld would occasionally put on a party for their employees, but only the more 'deserving' were allowed to go:

'The large annual parties that were given by Mr and Mrs Courtauld in their pleasure grounds, once or twice during each summer, when they had all sorts of amusements in the open air. Giving out the tickets on these occasions was always a trying thing, lest we should overlook the quietly deserving, or, admit the unworthy. We could not but see what moral weight such things had in our little community; the admission to these treats being held as a mark of respect and approval, understood and responded to by all alike.'   *Mary Merryweather*

Dances were sometimes held at the girls' lodging house. At first only married men with their families were invited, but later on single young men were permitted too. Eventually an Amusement Society was set up:

'Last summer there was so evident a want felt and expressed for some more extended and independent parties and amusements that the following rules for an Amusement Society were drawn up...'

These are some of the rules:

'That the parties shall take place on the first Wednesday of each calendar month. The amusement to commence at half past seven and conclude not later than eleven o'clock pm.

That refreshments, if required, will be provided at moderate charges excluding all intoxicating drink and tobacco.

That at each party, previous to the amusements three of the members present shall be chosen to act as stewards who shall be responsible for the good order of the company; and any member or members misconducting themselves, will be liable to expulsion.

The society had 245 women and 149 men as members, just over half of whom were employed at the Courtauld factory. According to Mary Merryweather, belonging to the society implied some status in the community:

'To belong to the Amusement Society implied a certain moral standing, and it was much sought by the young men and maidens. We have in some characters seen quite a reformation worked apparently by its agency.'

Another venture was a lending library for the women:

'One of the earliest efforts we made was establishing a lending library. It was at first intended for the women and girls, though some men and more boys availed themselves of it.' It contained 400 volumes, which for a long time circulated very constantly, and at last was added to the Factory Institution Library when women were received as members there.'

The women's reading interests are described:

'They preferred those also printed in large type, and those broken up into short chapters. Many a poor women has come regularly for a book for her "master" as she called her husband, who could not herself read a word, but begged me to give her a "pretty one".'

For the men, a Literary Institute was provided by Samuel Courtauld. This was not a lending library for taking books home like the women had, but was a place for the men to go to get away from their wives and children during the evenings.

'But there was great need, in such a community, for some place where a man should have the opportunity of reading the news comfortably, without having to spend his evening at the public-house. It could scarcely be in his own home, where probably his wife, just returned from her day at the factory, had to wash and scrub.

They were promised by Mr Courtauld if they would form themselves a Literary Institute, the principal means of carrying such a plan into execution, namely, a good-sized room near the factory, suitably fitted up with books, maps, etc. also a stove and necessary fuel; gas should be laid on, and supplied free of cost to the Society.

A room was provided near the factory, and there was an enthusiastic response at first, until the members discovered that they could not borrow the books:

'One hundred and one members enrolled themselves the first quarter, but from some misunderstanding about the books not circulating, which they had been expecting would have been allowed to do so, considerable bad feeling was evinced, and many withdrew, so that at the end of the year there were only fifty-three members.'

TO THE POWER LOOM WEAVERS.

HALSTEAD, MONDAY, MAY 21st.

To the Power Loom Weavers,

          Yesterday (Sunday Morning), I received a letter from Mr. Samuel Courtauld, which I at once print for your information, and at the same time I also place before you a telegraphic message sent by him, before he knew that you had left your work.

WILLIAM DAVIDSON.

Telegraphic message from Mr. Samuel Courtauld, received May 16th, at 12.30 p.m.

" BOURNEMOUTH.

      " I am in bed with sore throat. If there is any dissatisfaction, I will meet the Hands as soon as I am well enough,—I hope in a few days; meanwhile they should continue quietly at their work, but need not take out particular canes they don't like. It will grieve me very much if they are so foolish and so wrong as to do otherwise, and will oblige us in the end to discharge those who now mislead the well-disposed."

Letter from Mr. Samuel Courtauld, received May 20th, at 7.30 a.m.

BOURNEMOUTH, MAY 17th.

To William Davidson, Esq.

MY DEAR SIR,

        I am deeply grieved by the folly, and the bad spirit, shown on this occasion by the Halstead Power Loom Hands.

      The regulation of prices for some particular works was shown to be most reasonable; at the same time we made the acceptance of those works perfectly voluntary; no one was obliged to take out those works who preferred other works, and in fact we should care but little whether many of those works were made, or not.

      Nevertheless, we should have been, as we always have been, quite ready to listen to, and to fairly consider, whatever the Hands might have to represent to us in a proper spirit for our consideration, and we confidently believe we should have been able to satisfy them of the reasonableness and propriety of our regulations.

      They have, however, chosen to at once *strike*, and have by *that hostile and injurious*, but at the same time in the present case *most wanton and unfitting*, and certainly, as they will find, MOST VAIN ATTEMPT AT INTIMIDATION, made it impossible for us to confer with them in the friendly spirit in which they must know in their hearts we have always acted towards them.

      Under these circumstances we can have nothing whatever to say to them. While they are out they are no work-people of ours, and I will not meet them as though they were,—even when I may be well enough to leave this place, which at present I am not.

      On Monday morning you may get the steam up, and the Hands may resume work if they please; if they come in, well and good, and let me have the names of the first 50 who do so come in. If by the breakfast hour they do not come in, close all the Factories for the whole week. And if by the end of that week they still chose to be idle, we shall then take instant and vigorous measures to get a large portion of our goods at all events, permanently made in other parts of England.

      Of absolute necessity the Mills and Winding must stop, if the Looms stop, and however painful it is to us to stop the Mills and Winding for no fault of the Hands therein employed, we cannot in this case help it.

      Meanwhile, report to me the names of from 20 to 50 of those who have been foremost in this shameful disorder, for immediate and absolute discharge.

Yours very truly,

SAMUEL COURTAULD.

N.B.—Not having received Mr. Courtauld's letter in time to make known that the Looms would resume work on this (Monday) morning, or else be closed for the week, I now name Tuesday, at Two p.m., as the time at which they will so resume or be closed.

WILLIAM DAVIDSON.

This notice tells us about the strike of 1860

5 The workers' resistance

Women resisted the influence of Samuel Courtauld in many ways, from refusing to use the facilities made available to them to burning the rules of the lodging house. These kinds of protest were not organised or planned. In addition, there were two occasions on which the women joined together to oppose Samuel Courtauld.

In May 1860 women took strike action because the firm wanted to speed up production. Because of the piece-rate system this meant that women would have to work faster to get the same wage. Samuel Courtauld felt secure in the knowledge that the strike would be lost, and refused to meet the women, making an excuse that he was ill in bed. Furthermore Samuel Courtauld locked them out, threatened to dismiss the leaders and to move his mills to another part of England. The women were not in a union and there was no national movement prepared to help them. Samuel Courtauld was thus able to dismiss between 20 and 30 women because they were considered to be strike leaders. However, he took most of them back later because he needed them to work in his factory.

By the 1890s the Transport and General Workers' Union had attracted many silk workers into their union. In 1898 the weavers at Halstead were told to clean their own looms which they refused to do. It had always been the custom to have boys or men to clean their looms, and this new rule would have meant a loss of earnings, because the women were paid piece rates. Courtauld locked the women out of the factory, but the women held firm. They held a series of meetings at which the main speaker was Mrs M Brodie, of the Lancashire Weavers and Spinners Association and Womens Trade Union League. A large meeting took place on Market Hill beside the fountain which had been erected by Courtauld. The women decided to support the strike and called the men to help them.

Here are some extracts from reports that appeared in the Essex County Standard, West Suffolk Gazette and Eastern Counties Advertiser on Saturday, 18 June 1898.

SERIOUS LABOUR DISPUTE AT HALSTEAD

MESSRS S. COURTAULD AND CO'S FACTORIES CLOSED

About 1,300 weavers locked out
We regret exceedingly to have to record the outbreak of a labour dispute at Halstead, in connection with which the silk factories of Messrs S. Courtauld and Co. have been closed and about 1,300 weavers, mostly women and girls, have been locked out.

THE CORRESPONDENCE BETWEEN THE EMPLOYEES AND THE FIRM

Meetings have been held by the employees during the past week with Mrs A. Marland Brodie, of the Lancashire Weavers' and Spinners' Association and Workwomen's Trade Union League, and the following resolution was forwarded to the Managing Directors of the firm.

"WOMEN'S TRADE UNION LEAGUE" –

'That we, the employees at Messrs Samuel Courtaulds and Co.'s desire an interview with the Board of Directors on the question of cleaning looms, as we are unable to come to satisfactory terms with Mr Carter, the manager. Our case is this:
1 It has always been the custom to have boys or men to clean the looms. We are informed that we, the weavers, must clean the looms in future; this we decidedly object to as the work we are asked to do is not women's work at all.
2 Every Saturday we are asked to clean out looms for half-an-hour, and we were told we should receive twopence [2d] per loom for doing so. We have already cleaned the looms, but have had no pay for it. In this instance we also consider twopence per loom insufficient for the labour expended.'

Mr S. A. Courtauld sent the following reply:
'To the weavers at Halstead factory'

'We are this morning in receipt of the letter of the 9th inst., addressed to Mr George Courtauld, informing us of a resolution passed at a meeting of your Committee on the previous evening.

In reply we have only to inform you that as we understand that many of the weavers this morning refused to clean their looms, we have decided to close the factory entirely until further notice.

We very much regret having to take this course, because we have reason to believe that many of our weavers are quite ready to conform to our rule, but under the circumstances we cannot do otherwise. We shall be willing to re-open the factory when a sufficient number of weavers inform Mr Carter that they are desirous of resuming work according to our regulation.'

Mrs Brodie spoke from the fountain on Market Hill for a considerable time, urging the workpeople to stand out stoutly for what she considered their rights, and reproached the men of Halstead with having less pluck than the women. Before eleven o'clock an official notice was also posted on the factory lodge stating, 'These factories will be closed for the present until further notice, in accordance with the terms of a letter addressed by the Directors today to the weavers. By order of the Directors, & C'.

A Sunday meeting, on the Market Hill
On Sunday the streets were thronged with the workers discussing the situation, and in the afternoon an open air meeting held on the Market Hill was very largely attended. Mrs A. Marland Brodie, who was the principal speaker, said they abominated strikes and lock-outs.

A successful open air meeting had been held at Braintree, and when the weavers there were asked if they were willing to come and take the places here at Halstead they replied 'No' with one voice. (Hear, hear). She believed the factories had been closed to frighten the women, but they were not all made of the same stuff (hear, hear). She was glad they had some of a different spirit at Halstead. They thought their letter was written to the directors in a spirit that would have brought back a different reply. When the women asked the Union for advice, they were told, 'Don't do other people's work unless you are well paid for it, and don't do it at all if you throw anyone else out of employment'. They would stand by that.

The following resolution was put to the meeting and carried without a dissentient:

'That this meeting is of opinion that it would be unwise to return to work until some satisfactory arrangement has been arrived at, and further,

that they instruct the Committee to enter into negotiations with the firm forthwith.'

Again speaking, Mrs. Brodie said she believed there were women in that district who would go to prison before they would submit to their rights being violated. It would be better to be in prison than to be working in the factory, and doing work that never was intended for women. They wanted the men to stand by the women. (A voice – 'They haven't the pluck').

Samuel Courtauld won this dispute at the cost of a two-week stoppage. However, in later years, as the trades union movement became stronger and better organised, Courtaulds had to listen to the workers' demands.

A trade union poster encouraging silk workers to join the TGWU

Glossary

abominate	to loathe or dislike very strongly	mourning dress	black clothes worn as a sign of grief after the death of a close relative
admonitions	warnings		
almsgiving	giving money to the poor	negotiation	discussion, trying to settle a dispute by bargaining
amelioration	improvement		
appropriate	to get, acquire	nurse (baby)	to feed or look after a baby
attire	dress	parlour	a room for receiving guests
aversion	a dislike, unwillingness	patent	a licence granting sole right to make and sell an invention
bobbin	reel on which the silk was wound after spinning		
chiffon	transparent silk fabric	paternalistic	behaving in a fatherly fashion
clerk	person who works in an office keeping records and accounts	penury	poverty
		piece-rate	work paid for by the amount of work completed, or pieces produced
consumption	a disease called tuberculosis (TB) caused by bacteria that affected the lungs in particular		
		precosity	early or forward development
crape	thin cloth with wrinkled surface used for making mourning clothes	range	fireplace, used for cooking with oven
		restoratives	medicines
crepe	fabric other than crape with wrinkled surface made chemically or by twisting the thread	rood	a measurement of land, quarter of an acre
		silk throwing	preparing and twisting silk into threads
crimping machine	one that pleats silk	spindle	steel rod used for twisting and winding thread onto a bobbin
crepe de chine	very fine silk crepe		
crepon	a crape fabric with fluted or crinkled effort		
		sundry	various, several
dissentient	an objection or differing opinion	textile	material
		thrift	being careful with money
drawer	a person who operates a machine for lengthening and thinning yarn	want	lack of something
		waster	someone who looks after the waste silk that was collected and re-used
domestic servant	one who works in someone else's house as a servant	winder	a spinner of silk
economic necessity	the need for money	winding	a technical term for silk spinning
gauze	thin see-through fabric that can be of silk, cotton, or wire		
		unweaned	a baby that is still fed on breast milk
Huguenots	French protestants	vaccinate	to give someone a mild version of a disease (e.g. cowpox) so they do not catch the more serious form (smallpox)
idiom	a local term of speech or language		
licence	permission granted by an authority		
looms	machines for weaving thread into cloth	violate	disregard or break your word or promise
Justice of the Peace	a magistrate		

Case studies

Name	**Mary Ann Payne**
Born	**1845**
Place of Birth	**37, Chapel Hill, Halstead**

Home life

Mary lived with her mother, father, sister and three brothers. Her father, Isaac, and her eldest brother all worked as farm labourers. Mary's mother, Sarah Payne, worked at the Halstead mill as a crape weaver.

Factory life

Mary began work as a winder at the mill in June, 1858 at the age of 13. She was paid about 2s a week. Mary later became a weaver and earned between 5s 6d and 8s a week. Although Mary left the mill in August, 1873 'on account of her third illegitimate child' it is not known whether she was dismissed.

Later life

An attempt to get her job back in January, 1882 was unsuccessful and the records at Courtaulds say that Mary 'refused, left, impertinent and laughing'.

Questions on Mary Ann Payne

Home life

1 Find the photograph of the kind of house Mary Ann would have lived in and read the description on pages 7 and 10. Make a list of the home comforts in the house; make a list of all the things you consider uncomfortable.

2 Look at the rents for Courtauld's housing given on page 10. Look at Mary Ann's wages (page 17). When could she have afforded to rent her own cottage?

Factory life

1 Look at the table of male and female jobs (page 17). Which two jobs did Mary Ann Payne do? What was the job most commonly done by women? How many women managed to get better jobs than this?

2 Look at the rules that applied to women in the factories. Considering the description of Mary Ann Payne, what sort of things might she have done to disobey the rules?

Social life

1 Look at the picture of women workers on page 20. How would Mary Ann have dressed for the factory?

2 Make a list of the leisure activities provided by Courtaulds for women. Which ones, if any, might Mary Ann have enjoyed? Give reasons.

3 Read the reports on women's behaviour on page 22. Make up a report that might have been written about Mary Ann.

4 Look at the 1861 Census on page 7. Which relative of Mary Ann's was dismissed in 1850 and why? (page 22).

5 What arrangements were there for children:
a provided by Courtaulds?
b provided by the women themselves?
Which do you think Mary Ann would have preferred and why?

Resistance to authority

1 What could have prevented Mary Ann from going to work in May, 1860?
2 Do you think Mary Ann was one of the people who were discharged?
Why did she later leave?

Name	**Frederick Fawkes**
Born	**1827**
Place of Birth	**Trinity Road, Halstead**

Home life

Frederick married Mary in about 1848 or 1849 and had two children: Clara born in 1850 and Frederick born in 1852. Mary worked as a winder in the mill and she continued working after she got married and when she had her family. She too got promoted to the job of assistant overseer. Mary's mother lived with them and probably looked after the children while the parents were at work.

Factory life

Frederick started work at the mill as a winder at the age of 12. In 1841 he began to train as an assistant overseer. By 1852 he earned 11s per week – which was 3s more than the maximum that either a weaver or female assistant overseer could earn. (Women could not become overseers but only assistants to the men). By 1855, Frederick 'took charge of the winding floor in the New Mill building' at a wage of 16s per week. Then in 1862 he was 'promoted to the post of assistant overseer in the warping room' with an increased wage of 17s a week. In 1868 he received his final promotion to the position of principal overseer in the warping room at 27s 6d (£1 7s 6d) per week.

Later life

We do not know how much longer Frederick stayed at the mill. He died in 1872 after a week's illness.

Questions on Frederick Fawkes

Home Life

1 Look at the picture of the kind of house that Frederick lived in when he was an overseer. Compare this with the weavers' cottages. What differences do you notice?

2 Why do you think Frederick lived in one of the better houses?

3 Read the Housing Commissioner's Report on page 10. It describes two types of housing. What are they? Which type did Frederick live in?

4 What can you discover about the housing from both the Report and the photograph?

Factory Life

1 Look at the table on page 17 showing the model careers of men and women workers. Which jobs did Frederick actually do?

2 We do not know exactly what happened to Frederick in his old age. Give three things that could have happened to him. (Use the diagram on page 21 to help you.)

3 As an overseer, Frederick was one of the best paid men. What did he earn? How does this compare with the best paid women? (See table on page 17.)

Social Life

Look at the evidence about men's leisure activities in Mary Merryweather's Diary. In what various ways might Frederick have spent his time?

Resistance to authority

1 What job was Frederick doing during the strike of 1860?

2 Look at the last two lines of the letter addressed to William Davidson (page 32). How might Frederick have helped Mr. Courtauld to suppress the strike?

Name	**Emma Nelson**
Born	**1843**
Place of Birth	**Parsonage Street, Halstead**

Home Life

Emma had an elder sister Caroline, who in 1861 was 20 years old. She too worked in the mill. Emma also had a younger brother Walter, aged 10, who helped his parents at home, and a sister Frances who was 6 and went to school. Between 1861 and 1869 Emma's parents moved to London. In February 1869 Caroline left the mill to join her mother. Records tell us that Caroline had 'Gone to London to mother – Husband killed in street'.

Factory Life

Emma started work in the mill in December 1860. Her parents both worked at home weaving. It was better for Emma to work in the mill because she could earn a steady wage. Emma was a weaver and at the same job until she left eight years later. During her employment she earned between 6s and 8s a week.

Later Life

Emma left the mill in December in 1868 and is recorded as having 'left the town'. We do not know whether she got married or why she went. She might have gone to join her parents, or into domestic service which was better paid. The girls would often not say if they were going into domestic service because they knew that Courtaulds would not have them back, so they gave another reason like getting married. After 1869 we do not know what happened to Emma.

Questions on Emma Nelson

Home Life

1 Read the diary extracts describing weavers (like Emma's parents), working at home (pages 11 and 12). Now read the description of factory conditions on page 13. Where would you have preferred to work? Give reasons.

2 Both Emma's parents did weaving at home. What other jobs did Emma's mother do in the home besides weaving?

3 Draw Emma's family tree, showing each person's job. How many people worked for Samuel Courtauld?

4 How might Caroline's husband have been killed in the street?

Factory Life

1 Look at the pattern of women's work on page 21. How did Emma's working life start differently from most girls?

2 Find a picture of the machine that Emma would have worked. In which ways do you imagine you would feel tired after working this machine all day?

3 What sorts of things might Emma have been fined for as a weaver? (see pages 17 and 18).

4 Which machine was Emma and the other women not allowed to use? What do you think the real reason was?

Social Life

1 How old was Emma when her parents left? Where could single women like Emma live?

2 Look at the rules of the lodging house. What happened to the rules? If you were one of the girls, which of the rules would you have objected to and why?

3 What kinds of leisure activitities were available to Emma? Which ones do you think would have been most popular?

4 If Emma was sick, what could she do? (Pages 26 to 29). How was this paid for? From the evidence given here, would she have received good treatment?

5 Where might Emma have received an education? What would she have learnt?

Resistance to authority

1 Why might Emma have gone on strike in 1860? What was the outcome of the strike? What did Courtauld threaten to do if the workers went on strike? Which other workers in the factory were affected by the strike?

2 The strike was unsuccessful, but why do you think Emma left five years later?

Name	**William Root**
Born	**1846**
Place of Birth	**Halstead**

Home life

William's father, Benjamin, was a coalyard labourer, and his mother Susannah, was a crape worker at Courtaulds. There were three other children in the family, Ann who was born in 1853, Thomas in 1859, and Benjamin in 1861. William's mother was about 22 when she had him. In spite of having all these children, William's mother carried on working. Her children were probably looked after by relations or a young girl for about 1s 6d a week.

Factory life

William was about 13 years old when he started work as a winder in October, 1859. William only stayed until he was 15, when he was probably dismissed. Some of the boy winders were kept on to be trained for the more skilled jobs of overlooking or tending the machines. We know nothing about his later life.

Questions on William Root

Home life

1 Find the photograph of the kind of house William might have lived in and describe it.

2 His father, like many men at Halstead, did not work in the factory. Look at the map on page 9 and make a list of all the jobs the men might have done.

Factory life

1 Look at the poster about the little boys on page 16. Explain what happened to boys like William when they were 15 and why.

2 Look at the picture of the winding room and imagine you are a 13-year-old boy winder. Describe what it was like in the room.

3 How many boys worked as winders in 1861? (Page 17). What possibly helped William get a job?

4 Look at the picture of the crimping machine which was only worked by men. We don't know why this was so; can you think of any good reasons?

5 Make a list of jobs that only men could do. Can you think of any reasons for this? Are women capable of doing these jobs? What do you notice about the way wages for these jobs compared with the pay for the women's jobs?

Social life

Look at the picture on page 20 of the mechanics in the factory who would have been William's friends and neighbours when he grew older. These were respectable skilled workers. Look closely at the picture and comment on the following:
  health
  cleanliness
  dress.

Resistance to authority

In 1860, William's mother had to decide whether or not to go on strike. What family circumstances did she have to consider?

Further study

Men and women at work

Courtaulds is an outstanding example of a factory employing mainly women, but where a small number of men occupied the best paid jobs.

Write as much as you can about the working lives of men and women at Courtaulds. Use the following to help you: the table of jobs on page 17 and page 21. What do you notice about the jobs they did and the wages they received?

Find out from Mrs Merryweather's diary the reasons why women worked in the factory (pages 3 and 5).

Look at the map on page 9 to see what other jobs were available at Halstead.

Samuel Courtauld set up his factory at Halstead and preferred to employ women rather than men.

a Why do you think this was so?

b Why do you think the women worked in the factory rather than on the land?

How Samuel Courtauld got the best out of his workers

The evidence in chapter 4 shows that outside the factory there was much stronger control of the women's lives than of the men's.

1 Look carefully at the evidence about factory life (chapter 3) and social controls (chapter 4) and describe all the ways in which Samuel Courtauld attempted to control the women's lives. How far were men controlled in the same way?

2 Why do you think Samuel Courtauld was so concerned about the workers' lives outside the factory?

Resistance to authority

The Courtaulds workers took industrial action twice – in 1860 and later in 1898. In 1860 the Halstead workers were not in a union, but by 1898 they were included in a powerful union called the Transport and General Workers Union.

1 In each incident, explain briefly:

a Why action was taken.

b What the women did.

c How Courtauld reacted to the situation.

2 What are the main differences you can see between the events of 1860 and 1898 at Courtaulds?

Sources

Quoted

Census Enumerators Return 1861
Courtauld company records at Essex Record Office
Essex County Standard, West Suffolk Gazette, and Eastern Counties Advertiser 18 June 1898
Government Commission's Report on Housing, 1867
Merryweather M. (1862) *Experiences of Factory Life* Emily Faithful Publishing Company
Royston Pike E. (1969) *Human Documents of the Industrial Revolution* Allen and Unwin
Thompson E. P. (1968) *The Making of the English Working Class* Pelican

Used for reference

Local History Society *A Pictorial History of Halstead and District*
Coleman D. C. (1969). *Courtaulds: An Economic and Social History Vol. 1* Oxford
Hopkins E. (1979) *A Social History of the English Working Class* Arnold
Vicinus M. (1980) *Suffer and be Still – Women in the Victorian Age* Methuen
Courtaulds Ltd *Courtaulds – A Brief History*